WALKING
LIKE A GIANT

WALKING LIKE A GIANT

The Ultimate Guide to Surpassing Your Dreams and Realizing Your Destiny!

DAVID LAWHORN

MOUNTAIN ARBOR PRESS

MOUNTAIN ARBOR
PRESS
Alpharetta, GA

Although the author has made every effort to ensure that the information in this book was correct at the time of first publication, the author does not assume and hereby disclaims any liability to any party for any loss, damage, or disruption caused by errors or omissions, whether such errors or omissions result from negligence, accident, or any other cause.

ISBN: 978-1-63183-551-3 - Paperback
eISBN: 978-1-63183-552-0 - ePub
eISBN: 978-1-63183-553-7 - mobi

Library of Congress Control Number: 2020913652

Printed in the United States of America   0 8 0 7 2 0

⊗This paper meets the requirements of ANSI/NISO Z39.48-1992 (Permanence of Paper)

CONTENTS

Preface   vii

Introduction   ix

Chapter 1:
Welcome to the Land of Giants!   1

Chapter 2:
All Things Giant   11

Chapter 3:
Core Dynamics   17

Chapter 4:
Psychology 101   39

Chapter 5:
The Foundation   45

Chapter 6:
The Application! The Execution!   51

Chapter 7:
The Ultimate Sale! Selling Yourself to Yourself
and Others   57

Chapter 8:
Change   63

Chapter 9:
Take Your First GIANT Step!   69

Chapter 10:
YOU   71

Acknowledgments   95

This book is no ordinary book. It is powerful beyond measure, and if you allow the process to work, you walk away from this book with the ability to live any life you want to live. The copy of this book in your hands signifies that you share the one transformative that you can find at the core of every Giant. The one thing that wakes you before anyone else is up. That won't allow you to sleep, that constantly tugs at your core, at your soul. It screams you are not satisfied, not fulfilled, and that there is no rest until that one thing is manifested and made real.

That is why you have this book. The universe has felt that tug at your soul and is ready for you, my friend. IT IS YOUR TIME!

TO WALK LIKE A GIANT

Regardless of your current life position, there is something about you, something within you—gifts, talents, abilities—that when you commit to honing it, it will forever separate you from mediocrity. There is something within you, that if focused and evolved, will allow you to live life at a level that right now you only dream of. We all can live on that incredible level. Have you ever wondered, then, why so few of us do?

So few of us will ever get the chance to live life at that level because so few understand that to truly live YOUR LIFE, on THAT LEVEL, it must be a LIFESTYLE. Even fewer understand that there is *a price to access that dream lifestyle*. Contrary to what most like to think, the lifestyle you dream of living is not free. If it were, we would all be living it. This lifestyle, my friends, that you want so badly is on the other side of a fire that few are willing to endure. A fire that holds a promise that if you endure the flames, on the other side lie transformation and the gift of living your dreams.

This fire is fueled with a powerful transformative process that includes change, pain, and introspection, all feeding into a level of growth that allows you to tap into doing what most consider impossible and living on a scale that we all deem incredible. You are now reading my book because you know deep down, at your core, you were designed for more. That in fact, you are destined to live life on the scale of giants. You were made for this. All you need is either within you or waiting for you. Yes, my friend, it is your time. It is time for you to walk like a giant.

I want you to put everything else down and give this moment your undivided attention. The rest of your life depends on it! I then want you to go deep within. Now, think about all you have been at every stage of your evolution. Every experience, every win, loss, challenge, failure, defeat, everything that up to this very second has shaped and made up your life, made you who you are. Think about how it has all has come together to bring you to this moment, this game-changing moment where you have the extraordinary chance to not just live your dreams, but to live a life that surpasses your every dreams on every level—the life where you surpass your dreams and realize your destiny.

Today, you stop dreaming about that life. You start living it!

INTRODUCTION

I want this book to be a short, powerful, and impactful read. One that you will revisit from time to time throughout your evolution while understanding this principal: becoming a GIANT begins and ends with one core dynamic. FOUNDATION!

**"Do the same thing, you get the same results!
Do something different, change your thinking,
change your actions, you change your life forever."**

If you are in possession of this book, then understand this: you are in a unique holding pattern, a holding pattern in which every GIANT before you has found themselves at one time or another. A holding pattern that reminds you of the places you never want to revisit, a holding pattern that makes you take ownership of the fact that you have been going through the motions for far too long. You have been traumatized, you have witnessed loved ones suffer, and you now, in this moment, have your *aha* moment, the lightbulb moment that illuminates with stunning clarity that *only you* can change the situation.

THE POWER OF NOW

You will now come to understand the power of consistent, clarity-filled, focused action learning. To not act is not an option, because it means staying relegated to the land of not truly living, the land of just existing—and that, my friends, would be a life's greatest tragedy. You have cried out to the universe for opportunity, for just one chance to do on the stage of life that which is so vivid in your dreams. You made a declaration, declaring to the world just how badly you want it. Now understand this—when you cry out with that declaration, the universe will hear you. It will then test you, to see just how badly you want to live that dream inside of you. It is here that the lives of most will change in one of two ways.

While pursuing your dreams, you will be challenged like never before. The attacks will come relentlessly from all sides. You will be lonely to the point of despair. You will experience pain you would not wish on anyone. It is here that you will feel most misunderstood and utterly abandoned. It is here that you will feel the bitter taste of betrayal by those closest to you. It is here that you will tap into a place so deep within your core that you will give up food, sleep, and all you thought you had to have as you are consumed by an inner craving to taste your dream.

It is also here that you lose possessions, that your hunger intensifies. It is also here that the universe will demand payment for the greatness and lifestyle you seek. The bigger the dream, the bigger the payment. That payment comes in the form of insane sacrifice. I am talking about losing your car, or possible homelessness. You will give up time, friends, and yes, in some cases intimate relationships. It will change you, it will humble you, it will season you, so walking out of this, you will have a DECISION. It is here that most decide to give up, to settle for a safe and a dependable paycheck, not understanding that the price for that decision is a lifetime of regret.

But then you have that rare individual who has been tried and forged in fire, creating an unbeatable, unbreakable aura. An individual whose presence commands the room. The individual who, at that critical moment, decided to not give in, to not settle, but instead to understand that pain is for a moment, and regret will last a lifetime. This person understands that each challenge reveals something about yourself that will be critical in the days to come. You explore depth that has been there, but never tapped. You cross a line, a line that signifies you really are ready to take the walk culminating in living the rest of your life as neither man nor woman. We leave that title for those who gave up. You will live the rest of your life as a Giant!

For this book to create the level of transformation I intended when writing it, I need for you to start thinking not in terms of the old. From this point forward, the universe demands that your mode of thinking changes. As it changes, so will your life. I want you to answer the upcoming series of questions. They are geared to make you go deep within, to tap into your core, to grab answers and come up ready to work on doing what Giants do: SURPASSING YOUR DREAMS AND REALIZING YOUR DESTINY!

Question 1: What drives you?

What is your why? Your what? Your internal fuel? Is it:

- Family?
- Power?
- Achievement?
- Recognition?
- Safety?
- Order?
- Money?

It is critical that as you evolve you understand WHAT drives you and WHY. Those who excel at the highest level do so because they understand that even when you are not focused on the WHAT and why, the subconscious mind is the fuel that drives your decisions. It is those decisions that drive your actions, and ultimately those actions that decide your walk as a GIANT and your destiny.

Question 2: What would you do if you could only do one thing?

What is the one thing that if you died tomorrow would complete your life, one thing that you would do not for financial gain, but for the love of doing it because it satisfies that urge in your core? What would you do if you could take all chance of failure off the table and surprise even yourself? Life as you know it and the life that awaits you are waiting on the answer to this question. The answer will take you out of life as you know it, walking you step by incredible step into your ABSOLUTE best version of life. That is possible only when you tap into your absolute best version of yourself.

This is often the thing that provides us the most intense joy, yet also the thing the thing we hide in our deepest recesses, telling ourselves we are guarding our dreams as though they are our greatest riches. The reality is most of us guard that dream not only because of external doubts, but also the internal doubt within. Yes, in most of us, that self-doubt and fear is so great that it keeps our dreams insulated to the point that we never take that first step, which is why so many of us lead lives of misery and quiet desperation.

Question 3: What is the one habit you must kill off before it kills your dream?

We all have that one habit that is our Achilles' heel. I believe that habit is put there to test us, to see how badly we want that dream to become our destiny. To see what we are willing to forgo, give up, or overcome. BE HONEST!

Question 4: What is the one habit you MUST adopt in order to walk in the land of GIANTS?

Within each of us is one habit that, if adopted and implemented, will without a doubt become our GAME CHANGER! For you, is it:

- Discipline?
- Consistency?
- Commitment?

- Focus?
- Following through?

What is your MUST-HAVE HABIT?

***

Now that you have gone within and answered these questions, I invite you, whatever your current level, to ready your mind, so that you come away from this book WALKING LIKE A GIANT!

CHAPTER 1

WELCOME TO THE LAND OF GIANTS!

Life is either a daring adventure, or nothing.

—Helen Keller

What does it mean to LIVE and WALK LIKE A GIANT?

Giants are different, unique. Giants are out-of-the-box VISIONARIES. Their DREAMS, GOALS, and PLANS move with a flow and consistency that most can't grasp and perform immediate actions that are beyond incredible. The pure pursuit of their absolute best self along with a relentless, indestructible, fearless mindset yields astounding results, and makes what is impossible for most possible for you on every level.

To live and walk like a Giant means that you understand we get one life and that it is up to us to make that life the most phenomenal, regret-free experience possible, if only we commit to live our best version of ourselves.

Alex Honnold, Rock Star!

Alex Honnold is the best free solo climber on the planet! Free solo means that while most climbers have a partner and ropes, Alex climbs alone using no ropes or support systems. He has set records and made millions in endorsements climbing the world's tallest peaks. The money means he is secure, not that his life has changed. He drives and lives out of an old van. Alex is the purest essence of what is at the core of living and walking like a GIANT! For starters, he does the unthinkable, and in the process carves out not the road less traveled, but a new road entirely. Just think of what you will accomplish when you combine that kind of faith with an understanding of this program.

Welcome, Giant Nation!

I wanted this chapter to be two things.

First, I want to provide you with insight into who I am. Second, I want to highlight what qualifies me to act as your transformation catalyst, particularly in the realm of elite foundation strategies, the very strategies that separate average from GIANT. It is in this chapter that I will introduce you to what it means to be a GIANT.

I am David Lawhorn. All that I am will evolve from all I have been.

One thing I have never been is average. My life has always been a super high or a super low. Extremely good or very bad. I am from a family that has roots like the strongest tree. A good foundation is just like that good root. Those roots, that foundation, served me well. I was not only able to weather every storm, I was able to thrive in the mist of adversity. A great foundation allows you to overcome, it allows you to come back from what would cripple most, and it allows you to come out of each storm stronger, faster, and better.

The foundation we currently pull from takes shape in our childhood. My childhood was part heaven and part hell. The early years were heaven. My family lived an upper middle-class existence. My mother and father both enjoyed great jobs, and I can say that life was good. In our home, education was paramount, and that was key in laying those first, early layers of my foundation. When I turned twelve, there was a major shift that would profoundly shape the core of my foundation. First, my parents divorced. Their divorce was an ugly, epic battle in which there were no winners. The fallout from their divorce would affect my entire family for decades to come. The next life event occurred when my mom's health took a serious blow. A progressive heart and lung issue, coupled with deteriorating joints, confined her to home and took away any semblance of income. We found ourselves going from upper middle class, wanting for nothing, to being so poor there were days we didn't eat. Our lives changed from donating Thanksgiving food baskets to the less fortunate to then being thankful to receive those very same baskets in our own desperate need.

Seeing my family struggle to that degree, on that level, forever changed me as a person. Even now, to this day, it affects me. Seeing your mother go without good shoes or a good coat in winter changes you. There were so many lessons learned during that period of my childhood that shape who I am today. A powerful takeaway that resonates with me even now is that I can, and will, survive whatever challenges that might come my way. I also learned, with the level of absolute clarity that forever shapes your standards and acceptable living conditions, that there is a level of living I never, ever want to revisit.

BECOMING A TEEN FATHER

My life to most reads like a Hollywood script. At seventeen, I had two profound events occur. First, I was notified that I had been accepted into the fall freshman class of Morehouse College. This was a monumental milestone, as I would be the first in our house to attend college. Family pride was at an all-time high. That pride would soon turn to despair, because while on top of the world at the joy of attending Morehouse, I got the news I would become a teen father.

It's not if, but when we all will get the wind knocked out of us. In most cases it is the unexpectedness that makes the blow so devastating. Average people would falter here, not recover, and become a statistic. As a teen father I was determined to instead become an example of what your life could be like if you keep fighting in your darkest moments, when things are not going your way, when everyone around has given up. That if you push through those times—and this certainly qualified as one of those times—you will find you can overcome ANYTHING. Average people, in those moments of being on their knees, wind knocked out of them, will ask the universe, "Why me?" That question marks a victim. The question you should ask instead is the question that changes everything, the question that puts your power squarely back in your hands: WHY NOT ME? I instead asked, "WHY NOT ME? Why not me overcoming that challenge? Why not me whom the universe will make stronger for going through the fire?" In asking this, you open yourself up the lessons that lead to Giant steps.

ATTENDING MOREHOUSE COLLEGE

I was accepted and went on to attend one of the premier schools in the country, Morehouse College. Morehouse was critical in my evolution, and it provided a confidence that I carry to this day. Their process for turning boys to men is like no other on the planet. It is an incubator of the highest standard, allowing a glimpse of what success looks like at an international level. From day one, this standard is established and expected. It is this internal standard and fortitude that makes you a Morehouse Man.

I left college ready to take on the world. I would go out and get married, and a few years later I would get divorced. The marriage gave me a lot of insight into what happens when a relationship isn't nurtured and cultivated, even if you are great friends. It would take years before I fully understood what that meant. I think last year, I finally got it. I wanted to forge my way and make my fortune, but life decided it had a few lessons for me. Those lessons brought with them extreme highs and severe lows.

Determined not to go back to Mom's house, I would at my lowest find myself homeless.

SETTING NATIONAL SALES RECORDS

I found the world of sales by accident. At least, I thought it was an accident. I would later realize it was fate. I would go on to have a stellar sales career and break national sales records for several Fortune 500 companies. It was also here I was offered the opportunity to train and teach others the art and psychology of sales.

One decision, be it right or wrong, good or bad, has the potential to change your life forever. For some people, that decision might be a good one, as in the day they decided to say hello to their future husband or wife. For others it might be the decision to quit the job they hate and start their dream business. Then there are the decisions that hurt, devastate, and change us forever. Those decisions most never recover from.

GOING TO FEDERAL PRISON

I made one of those decisions. It turned out to be a life-changing mistake. A mistake that taught me there are two types of pain: the pain that hurts, and the pain that alters. Because of that mistake, the next six years would be the pain that alters. Because of that mistake, I would spend the next six years as a guest of the federal prison system. It was here in my darkest, loneliest, early days of that six-year journey that I had made what I came to realize later was my first decision as a GIANT. I had to decide I would not believe the noise that said when you get a criminal record, your life is over. Or the belief that a person's dreams die the day you are sentenced. I chose instead to believe that voice in my head and heart that told me I was different, that I could march to the beat of my own drum and walk the path less traveled. I decided that deep within I had a great foundation, and acknowledged I made a mistake. I decided if I wanted it, I could overcome this mistake and the many obstacles it would present. I chose to believe the voice within me that said, "YOU CAN DO THIS! YOU ARE A GIANT!"

TRANSFORMATION

I made a decision, a decision to turn what most considered impossible into the incredible. I decided I WOULD WIN! I never once thought that doing this, overcoming the challenges, hurdles, obstacles in my path, would be easy. Understanding the road ahead of me, I needed to devise a plan. I decided I would not allow prison time to do me; instead, I would do the time. I decided I would take advantage of every second of the next six years, and when got out I would shock the world while changing lives and perceptions.

While in prison, I filled my cell with books. In fact, I had more books than food. Over the next six years serving my sentence, I would read about one hundred books per year. I identified my strengths, making them stronger while cutting out everything I considered a weakness.

At that point, I had been a smoker for ten years. Most smokers say they tend to smoke more in times of stress, and I can't think of a place more stressful than federal prison. To stop smoking while in federal prison would be a huge test. Yet stop I did. I have not had a cigarette since 2002.

I decided to quit putting anything in my body that was not considered healthy. In my quest to become healthy, I started working out in the gym, and I started a habit that kept me sane. This is one habit I still practice today: meditating. I also taught business classes in the prison's education department. I even teamed up with a fellow inmate to offer a class on entrepreneurship.

The hardest thing about prison is there is no place to run or hide from your thoughts. You are forced to face some very hard truths. I had to face every decision I had made up to that point, and its consequences. It was not pretty. This process involved a lot of tears, anguish, and self-forgiveness. When done, I made myself a promise. I promised myself that when I got out of this prison, I would live life on a level most only dream of while teaching others all I learned while there.

YOU ALWAYS HAVE A CHOICE

My biggest lesson is that you always have a choice. Circumstances don't define who you are; what defines you is, in fact, how you handle those circumstances, and that belief in your choice is everything.

I decided to get stronger. That meant reading like never before, working out both my body and mind. It meant searching out and spending time with like minds. It meant eradicating weakness of any kind. Those around me could see the growth. There was a respect from inmates and staff alike that few others would have. I think that respect stemmed from my refusal to become or be average. Yes, I was in prison, but that did not mean I had to act like the stereotypical prisoner.

I am a drummer, so I started playing for various bands, including the classic rock band, the gospel group, the R&B group, and both American and Spanish church services. By year three I was in such a great mental space. I was being sought out for advice. At this point I cut back on family visits, not wanting them to endure the long drive. Just when I thought I had transcended and made a huge mental leap, I was then tested on an epic and tragic level. It was here that I suffered the tragic loss of my little brother, who was twenty-eight years old. I got the news of his death right after playing for a church service. I still see the room and hear the words that he had died the night before like it was yesterday. It rocked me to my core. This was one of the things I had been most afraid of—losing a close family member at any time—but especially in here. I was not allowed to attend his funeral, but I did send something that my remaining brother read:

"God will have you face your biggest fear just to show you that you are stronger than you think."

At this point I had hit a new level as I started to put in place the plans for my release and future business. I also understood this placed me in a select group. That I was now mentally stronger that 98 percent of the population. That I had just gone through and not just survived but thrived in conditions that would mentally break and destroy most. I was ready. On January 5, 2005, after spending 2,190 days as a guest of the federal prison system, I was coming home.

Coming home from prison was crazy. I had absolutely nothing to my name. No clothing, shoes, not even a toothbrush. My brother got me a starter kit of hygiene essentials, a set of clothing to go job hunting, and a few changes of clothing, and I was off. Nothing was easy. I would find my first job after being told no countless times. My first job was working for a family-owned barbecue restaurant. I did it all, from staking firewood, bussing tables, to sweeping floors, and I loved every second. That job put me in position to work on my strongest skill set: creating relationships. Within six months I was back in ground-floor sales. Six months after that I was working in marketing sales. I would work that job for two years, setting company and national records along the way. It was here I became a sales performance trainer. It was here I found my destiny.

**"Believe, prepare, act.
Then watch as the universe welcomes you."**

After two years, it was time for change. Time for the manifestation of the incredible out of the impossible. All it took was one person to say yes. Someone on a major level at a major said yes, that they would give me a chance. That chance was all I needed. That opportunity catapulted me into a position of change agent. As a trainer on a national level, I saw how I was able to effect change on so many levels. It was also here the seeds were planted for what would become my life, my business, and my brand.

The universe welcomed me back into the world of sales at a high level. In the span of twenty-four months, I went from prison to making six figures. There was still so much out there for me, so I went headfirst into the world of corporate training. I had done stints as both speaker and trainer before, but now I wanted to work on making it full time. That would mean getting serious on an entirely different level. In 2011, I would join Toastmasters, and I would go on to become a Toastmaster's District Leader and a two-time DTM (Distinguished Toastmaster), the highest designation you can earn. It was in Toastmasters that I entered and won speech contests with the thought process of competition making us sharper, stronger, and better versions of ourselves. I offered free speeches for years, learned a lot, and cried a lot, never losing sight that on the other side of this process I would get to live my dreams and explore everything I ever thought possible at the ultimate level. That ultimate level will differ for each of us. Your journey will show you what your version looks like to you. Your goal, then, is to evolve from your current self into the person who allows you to live and thrive on that level.

I now walk into this chapter with the confidence that comes with experience that would cripple most. I humbly stand where most never get the chance, at the summit of the mountain of my past. My passion, my mission, the why that I eat, breathe, and sleep is to reach, touch, and convert as many Giants around the globe as I can. The most exciting part of all is that we get to walk into this next chapter together.

"You were born for this."

Kyle Maynard

Kyle Maynard is a twenty-seven-year-old congenital amputee who has accomplished more than most able-bodied people will in their lifetime. Despite having had all four limbs amputated, he became a champion wrestler, competed as a mixed martial artist, and was even the first quadruple amputee to climb Mount

Kilimanjaro—the tallest mountain in Africa—by crawling up the entire 19,341 feet. He also owns a CrossFit gym in Georgia.

Maynard is an inspirational example of incredible inner strength and perseverance. Despite all the obstacles he has faced, he continues to defy the odds and do things that no one would have ever thought he could do.

Understand this—most of us look around at our surroundings and embrace everything but the courage and resolve to make our dreams real. You have heard it before: if it were easy, everyone would be living their dreams. We know that is not the case because so many of us live lives of misery. Why? Because we allow everyone and everything to occupy a sacred space. A sacred space that, when filled with the right people and things, allows you to do the amazing, live the incredible, and WALK LIKE A GIANT!

CHAPTER 2

ALL THINGS GIANT

This is your life.

This chapter is devoted to you—to who you currently are, to all you have overcome, and to the GIANT you are designed and destined to become. I want you to come away from this chapter feeling at your core the transformative powers at work and understanding the dynamics that make up the foundation found inside of every Giant. Yes, that means you! The foundation of every GIANT starts with an understanding of this fundamental truth, that each of us, no matter our past or potential, has something in common: We are all uniquely designed and different. We all have dreams. We all have incredible talents, gifts, and abilities. This chapter will allow you to grasp what makes GIANTS so profoundly different, what makes you so profoundly different, and how it all starts with the unmatched, unmistakable power springing from your core. I want you at the end of this chapter to have the ability to tap into the power source reserved for GIANTS and experience the extraordinary degree of separation that separates GIANTS from everyone else on the planet.

ALL THINGS GIANT

My fellow Giants understand there is a transformation from the current version of you to the polished version of living your dream. I want to provide you a glimpse of what your immediate future looks like. Everything is riding on whether you grasp the following pages of this book.

Giants understand that their habits are different.

Giants understand their abilities are different.

Giants understand that their expectations are different.

Giants understand they have different standards.

Giants are different at the core!

Which ultimately means that a Giant's lifestyle is drastically different, and that drastic difference makes you a GIANT!

Giants invented the term self-investment and are masters at investing in themselves.

HARD LOSS, HUGE WIN

I want to do something with this life of mine.
I want to take my life as a great opportunity that I can't waste.

—Alex Zanardi

Alex Zanardi, Racer X

Alex first made his mark on the racing world in Formula One cars. There he won two championships and became one of the most popular drivers in the world. In 2001, at the height of his career, Alex was involved in a horrific crash. He survived, but lost both legs. While the loss would have been a sure mental death blow for most, Alex, overjoyed to be alive, chose to show the world what GIANTS are made of. Not only did he recover, but he held on to that love of racing in his blood, so he searched for and found the perfect outlet in handcycling. Alex, who never did anything halfway, decided to challenge himself and enter a handcycling race. He developed an intense training program that tapped into the champion mindset and preparation used to win his multiple titles, and soon he was in racing form. He went on to compete and win the New York Marathon handcycling division. Did he stop there? NO! He topped that by winning three medals (including gold) at the Paralympics. His story is one that shows the never quit, never stop, never give up attitude at the core of every GIANT!

**"Change the way you look at things,
and the THINGS YOU LOOK AT WILL CHANGE."**

IT ALL STARTS WITH YOU!

Giants, welcome to the world of YOU! It is here you start the process where you, my fellow Giants, will gain insight into what it takes to grasp and live out the lifestyle of a GIANT. It is also here where we tear your life down to the studs, making some tough decisions that will forever alter how you see. This may lead to the circle of people and things surrounding you looking drastically different. You will lose a lot of what you love that may not be healthy, or in line with your DREAMS, as we start to build your BRAND AS A GIANT. I want you and I together to build and add value to every aspect of you. To build stronger and better so that your result is a level and scale you could only imagine. That big win is what we can now recognize as the base foundation of a GIANT!

**"The hardest work you will ever do
is the work you do on yourself."**

This chapter will challenge you like no other. Why? Because the most frightening dynamic we will ever face in our quest to evolve is OURSELVES. There is a billion-dollar industry designed around the intentional distractions we indulge in to avoid that honest look within. Because that look within can be so unsettling, this chapter has one focal point: introspection. You will find as you evolve, the ritual of introspection will become one of your most valuable and trusted tools. It is here, in this chapter, that we take a step back, tearing down in the process (hard loss) so you can then take a Giant leap forward (huge win).

Every prolific fiber in the foundation of a Giant begins, and ends, with a higher level of self-awareness. It is this awareness, and the layer of unbreakable foundation it creates, that will ultimately separate you, the Giant, from everyone else. This layer of foundation is probably the hardest to establish because it means looking at yourself and being brutally honest in ways most never will. In our makeup, there are so many layers. Those layers make up a compilation of the personas we develop and use with various individuals and in various situations.

Those personas are intended to serve us, acting as flavors accenting our powerful core selves. What happens instead, because the core self is not the powerful source it was designed to be, is that we start to cover over the weak core self and its layers until it becomes difficult to identify our true, authentic core. This is the version of life most of us live, and quietly hate. The core at this stage is a weak, unrecognizable shell of the powerhouse it is designed to be.

EXERCISE: HARD TRUTH

The first step in becoming all you will become is to face and accept all you currently are. True, authentic power comes when you are aware of how you got to this place in your life that you know should be so much better. Most of us run away, and never deal with the dynamics of our past including the bad and the ugly. We are never able to embrace 100 percent of who we are, and thus we are not able to grasp and take hold of the opportunities that can walk us into our absolute best lives.

I have an exercise for you. I call it hard truth. I want you to take the blank page provided for you in the back of the book and go to a place where you can quietly and honestly reflect. I want you to look at your life in the present, the right now, and ask yourself this question: Ten years ago, when I pictured myself at this point, what did that picture look like? What had I achieved, what lifestyle did I enjoy? Then I want you to write down all the reasons that add up to why you're not living that life. There is one rule: YOU MUST BE COMPLETELY HONEST! Did you procrastinate, was it a relationship, did you use a situation as an excuse? No matter how painful—and trust me, this process will be painful—I want you to give yourself over completely to this process. Again, our goal throughout this chapter is complete awareness and acceptance of where we are and who we are. That acceptance is the first step in liking, and more importantly, loving, who you are. This core concept is one of the most fundamental and most powerful that you possess in your evolution as GIANT.

Ready? GO!

POST-EXERCISE

Wow! I am willing to bet if you were 100 percent honest with yourselves during that exercise, you came away with an eye-opening perspective of what brought you here, to this point, your current life position.

THE MINDSET SHIFT

This is the last time I want you to ever look at your life with the regret of would've, should've, or could've been. Every Giant comes to a place and time when they face this, they get it, they understand that there is no going back. No do-overs. It is here that you get your most profound lesson in the POWER OF NOW. Giants are so powerful and have the clarity to do such phenomenal things because they understand yesterday is gone. Tomorrow is not promised, and the most incredible gift you will ever have is the gift of being fully present in the NOW. How many times have you heard that? How often do you live it?

In order to lay one of the most important layers of foundation you will ever put in place, I want you now to do something so profound, so powerful, something so simplistic, yet so hard for most of us to do. Once done, this act will open you up to the fullness of the possibilities this book was designed to have you explore and take advantage of.

I want you to forgive yourself.

FORGIVE YOURSELF

I want you to forgive yourself for all the mistakes you are ashamed of, for the decisions and choices that created the life you currently live. I know you have regrets you wish you could go back and change. I want you to stop beating yourself up. Walk into any room and look around—we all carry regret. Let yours go today. Free yourself of that weight. This step is critical because you cannot, *will* not, be able to claim your place as a Giant until you do this.

"This is your life."

CHAPTER 3

CORE DYNAMICS

Don't downgrade your DREAM just to fit your REALITY.
Upgrade your conviction to match your DESTINY!

—Anonymous

Tererai Trent, GIANT DREAMER!

She symbolizes everything I believe "GIANT" stands for. Her story encapsulates the essence of hope. She proves you can keep reaching for your dreams, that one person can make a difference in the world—and above all, you have the power. It doesn't matter where you come from.

I came across a story on Oprah.com that embodies the life and walk of a Giant: "As a young girl in rural Zimbabwe, Tererai lived without running water and electricity. Although she was desperate to learn, she only attended two terms of school before she was forced to marry at age eleven. In 1991, Tererai met a woman from Heifer International and told her what her greatest dream was: to move to America and get her PhD. The woman looked at Tererai and said, "If you desire those things, it is achievable." Tererai's mother later encouraged her to write her dreams down, so Tererai wrote them on piece of paper, placed them in a tin box, and buried them under a rock.

"By 1998, her dream started to come true. Tererai moved to Oklahoma with her husband and five children. Just three years later, she earned a bachelor's degree in agricultural education. In 2003—the same year her husband was deported for abuse—

Tererai obtained her master's degree. After every achievement, Tererai returned home to Zimbabwe, unearthed her tin of dreams, and checked off each goal she accomplished, one by one.

"Today, Tererai is happily remarried and had made the fourth dream that she wrote down come true as well—she was awarded her PhD!"[1]

"We are all faced with a series of great opportunities brilliantly disguised as impossible situations."

—Charles R. Swindoll

CORE DYNAMICS

Giant Nation. THIS. IS. YOUR. TIME! Your time to recognize your authentic powerful core, time to recognize your true opportunities. Your time is now, my fellow Giants, to decide to never again settle for average or less than you were destined for. Right here, right now is your time to evolve, your time to conquer doubts, your time to conquer fears, and your time to conquer obstacles. This is the time to discipline your undisciplined self. This, my fellow Giants, is your time to live your dreams!

Every letter of every word of every chapter of this book, the concepts and the signature program within, are the result of more than twenty years of questing and researching to discover and identify the following Core Dynamics that allow you to not just thrive, but actually live out your absolute best life.

You will find that these are infinitely powerful Core Dynamics that we all will have access to. At this point, I ask this question: Why is it so few of us can live out our dreams? The skills described in the Core Dynamics Program, when tapped and honed, will allow you to perform, produce, manifest, and

---

[1] "Oprah's All-Time Favorite Guest Revealed," Oprah.com, May 20, 2011, http://www.oprah.com/oprahshow/oprah-reveals-her-all-time-favorite-guest/6.

live at levels most people only dream of. The Core Dynamics Program works at its best when you understand the process and payoff, allowing you to become a part of the most elite tribe on the planet.

What is it that drives the elite? What is the degree of separation between good and great? I chose the term Core Dynamics to title my signature program because it totally encapsulates the concept of a foundation that allows you to do the incredible things, have the amazing lifestyle, and experience the universe as only Giants can. The universe will now open up for you because you are now ready for this transformation. Therefore, on behalf of all Giants, welcome to Core Dynamics!

THE SYSTEM

Core Dynamics is the system and platform making up the **foundation** and **epic core** of every Giant. The epicenter of this system is made up of three core pillars. That epicenter and those pillars are supported by the bricks that make up your life expectancies, the pain, the lessons, representing the process you go through from your current to future self and the essential dynamics found in the buildup of every Giant.

THE THREE CORE PILLARS

The three core pillars are the heartbeat of this system. Like your body, if your heart is out of sorts, so goes everything else. When looking at the three pillars of Core Dynamics, you will clearly see that powerful tie-in. My philosophy with these three pillars is that if you ever hope to do anything incredible, amazing, or phenomenal in your life, if you ever hope to truly walk where so few have walked, then these three pillars will have to be in place at a high level. If you look at any Giant on any level, in any arena, and they have one thing in common, it would be these three pillars. The stronger the pillars, the more incredible the lifestyle. The three pillars that form the cornerstone in the foundation of every Giant are:

1. Time Management
2. High Performance Levels
3. Personal Development

OVERVIEW

If you cannot effectively manage your time, you will never live out your dreams. It is that simple. Show me a lifestyle and I can show you how they use their time. The second pillar, High Performance Teams, is a must because you truly are only as good as the team around you. Anyone doing anything astounding starts and ends with a super team around themselves. If the team sucks and is subpar, so goes the dream. The Personal Development pillar might just be the most important and impactful of the three because it involves your mindset and the strengths and weaknesses of your mental makeup. Everything else can be in place at the highest of levels, but if your personal development is not where it needs to be, then you will never walk like the Giant you were meant to be.

PILLAR ONE
TIME MANAGEMENT

How you use your time will ultimately decide if time is your dream maker or your dream stealer. Which will it be for you? Most of us are so close to living our dreams. We have put in the work, the sweat, the tears, and now we are right there. But there always seems to be that one last hump that for some reason we can't quite get over. Have you ever thought your last hump and the inability to get over it might have everything to do with how you use and spend your time? There are 86,400 seconds in a day. Time is the one thing that no matter your education or economic level, we all get the exact same amount. The way you use and manage those 86,400 seconds in your day will, I promise, determine the quality of the rest of your life. It is why you see so many living such drastically different lives. There are three truths about time that every Giant holds sacred:

1. Time is unforgiving.
2. Time never stops.
3. You can never get time back once it has passed.

TIME IS UNFORGIVING

Use your time effectively and you won't just live out, you will surpass your most audacious dreams. If you don't use your time effectively, and waste time instead of respecting it, I promise you that you will live the worst life one can imagine. That life of wasted time—wishing for time to turn back, to give you another chance after life beats you down, until every part of you stands defeated—is the signature of how unforgiving time can be.

It is unforgiving because *time does not stop* to let you get your head right or give you back what you wasted or did not appreciate. It is fascinating when talking to the elderly and those who have terminal diseases that the one thing they want more of and work to make peace with is time. How they used it, how they misused it, and in the end, their reverence for it. On their death bed, no one ever wishes for more money, but they shed tears for time and the chance to say words that can't go unsaid, to touch a loved one once more or even right some wrongs as they take their last breaths. In the end, time—not money, my fellow Giants—will be the one thing you yearn for more of. Time is without question the most valuable and most underappreciated gift we will ever get.

Most of our troubles will come with how we see, recognize, and process our use of time. It is mind boggling how we take such exceptional care of everything else in our lives, including our cars, our homes, our bodies, and our money, because we consider these things valuable, while we'll be so careless with how we manage our time. It is not until that internal light goes off, illuminating and providing clarity, that our respect for a minute will forever change. It is there, at that moment, your life will hit its next Giant level.

TIME NEVER STOPS

Time is constant. Time is perpetual motion, and yes, my friends, the older we get the more we understand that time never stops, regardless of whether we move with it. Funny how when we're young we beg time to speed up so we can enjoy the fruits of being a grown-up, but when we do grow up, we beg time to slow down as days become weeks, weeks months, months years, and the one that really hurts, years becoming decades. No matter who we are or what we do each day, two profound things take place. The first is the raw gift of the fresh canvas the new day brings, and the extraordinary opportunity it presents for us to manifest our dreams. The second profound thing that happens each day is we recognize from the moment we are born, we start the process of dying. Our bodies age by the minute. While we can't stop this, we can forever see time through perspectives that allow us to then manage the processes that determine how we can maximize the phenomenal gift of time.

YOU CAN NEVER GET TIME BACK

It is my sincerest wish as you evolve into the unique Giant you were destined to become that you also become one of the rare 2 percent. Ask most people, when they realize their days are numbered, what their one wish is regarding time. Most will tell you because the sum of their life went by so fast, they wish they could get more of it. Most wish they could have used their time better, and they wish they could get just another moment with a friend or loved one who has died so they can share words or heartfelt thoughts they never had the chance to. Thing is, no matter how hard we wish, once the moment has been spent, we never can get back. Not even a moment. My question for you, then, is how you will choose to live the rest of your life. Stark reality makes us all face that we die each day, and in the midst of dying, we can choose to simply exist or do the impossible and live the incredible.

THE DREAM STEALERS:
WHAT IS STEALING YOUR TIME AND
ROBBING YOU OF YOUR DREAM!

DISTRACTIONS

Your dream is being held hostage! When you look at the chief reason so many of us never live out our dreams, why so many of us are so miserable, and why so many of us never walk like the Giants we were created to be, it comes down to the ultimate, one-word dream stealer: **DISTRACTIONS!** So many of us put in hundreds of hours figuring out just where our dreams came off the rails. If you are reading this, it means the universe has decided that while you may think you are doing great, you are not living your dream and thriving. After this chapter, you will understand the destructive force that has you living in your current state, and in doing so, change the rest of your life. You will understand how, despite having everything look so incredible on paper, we still end up failing, and why most of us never live those dreams.

My friends, there is a no single word that has sent more dreams to the graveyard, unfulfilled, than distractions. It is so deadly because it is so often overlooked. It has outsmarted the smartest, it has dethroned kings, it has taken away superpowers, and it will leave you broken. Because it comes at us in so many disguises, often by the time we recognize them for what they are, it is too late.

Now that you know what distractions do, let's talk about what they are.

We are going to break down top dream-stealing distractions into two categories: 1) what is stealing your time, and 2) who is stealing your time.

What Is Stealing Your Time?

Dream Stealer #1: Cell Phone

There have been few inventions in the history of mankind that have had the profound effect of our top dream stealer. The insane thing is that this device was created to destroy any remaining barriers standing between you and you living your most audacious dreams, your best life. It was also created with an even bigger mission in mind: to bridge gaps in our communication and make our relationships stronger than ever. This is the device, my friends, that was designed to make you superhuman! It is the one device we own that, since its inception, has changed our world on every level. It is also the single device more than any other that steals so much of your quality time, relationships, and memories. If you haven't guessed yet, that device is . . . *drum roll* . . . your CELL PHONE!

Yes, my fellow giants, that's right! The very invention designed to make you more productive, your cell phone, and the invention that improves beyond measure the quality of your relationships, the device designed to level up your life, is the very device that now holds you prisoner, that has you so busy doing nothing that without realizing it, you are being robbed. Robbed of your focus, robbed of your drive, robbed of your best relationships, robbed of memories, robbed of your dreams, robbed of your ability to walk like a giant.

This one device is killing the quality of your relationships and draining the essence of your moments. How many times have you attended an epic concert or event, only to see most missing the fullness of the moment because they are too focused recording the moment with their phones? How many of us are guilty of having an important conversation and at the same time navigating our phones? My friends and fellow Giants, heed this warning—one day you will wish, with all that you are and own, for a chance to have just one more moment with that person you took for granted. The device will always be there, but those you love and appreciate you will never get back to you once they are gone. We all are guilty at some point of doing all the above. In moving forward, understand that if we change the behavior and experience, the intense joy you were supposed to receive will instead be filled with the emptiness that overwhelms most of us.

You want to give yourself a priceless gift, a gift that will enrich your life and the lives of those around you, so learn to manage your phone and not allow it to manage you. It will change your life!

> *Mind Shift:* Most of us have this idea that the pain associated with missing a call or not instantly responding to a call or text will kill us. We are under the impression that if we don't get that picture or video at an event that we have missed out on something. We fail to realize it is those very actions that rob us of fully capturing moments. We think if we are not going through our various apps, something will escape us. My friends, I can assure you that you will not miss anything, and that you will live! In fact, not only will you live, you will thrive.
>
> Giants have a perception of their surroundings that makes them different at the core. I want you to shift the way you make and respond to calls. Shift the way you utilize your cell phone overall and create a game-changing momentum shift in your life. The Giant mind shift involves adopting a new, simplistic, yet hugely impactful and disciplined regimen. The mind shift you make here has everything to do not only with the time you create by changing behaviors, but also what you do with the time you would

normally allocate for phone activities. This could be as simple as setting clearly defined, hard-line boundaries such as setting up a voicemail so you can screen calls. This allows you to cut out any calls that disrupt the critical workflow that manifests your dreams. You can do what you have been doing and get the same results, or you can do what Giants do and take full advantage of the gift of freed-up time.

Dream Stealer #2: Email

The culprit that holds the distinction of being number two on my list of dream-stealing distractions is none other than your EMAIL!

How many times have you jumped out of bed, excited and giddy that you are about to conquer your day and manifest your dreams? You planned each step of your day with meticulous care the night before and feel unstoppable. THEN YOU CHECK YOUR EMAIL!

In an instant, all of the well-laid plans you were so excited about go out the window. All it takes for most of us to have our entire day derailed is that one well-placed email that seems so urgent and demands our undivided attention. It is at that point that any hope of your day being recovered is lost. It is not until the day is gone and you are preparing for bed that you realize with utter dismay you lost an entire day. Yes, you may have put out fires, you may have even been productive, but you did not WORK ON YOUR DREAM.

This is the vicious, debilitating, dream-stealing cycle most of us unknowingly find ourselves in. The crazy thing is that at some point we see and recognize this cycle for what it is, yet we are unable to make the changes needed to prevent this crippling pattern and, in the process, change our lives. How do we break this cycle?

Mind Shift: You break this cycle by understanding that the point of your greatest despair comes with realizing your dreams are slipping away. It is, in fact, this point that holds your greatest potential. There is a process here that I can sum up for you with one phrase, that when grasped and utilized will transform your life on every level. That process is DISCIPLINE.

Here is where you change the habits that change your life. The major habit you change is how you view and answer emails differently going forward. The discipline comes with resisting the urge to view emails randomly. Instead, employ a window that we will call a **power break.**

The dynamic that makes a **power break** work is the discipline associated with how badly you want it. How badly you want change. How badly you want that life you can almost reach out and touch, turning your dreams into your reality. How badly you want to present your best version of yourself to the world. Today, social media is the newest and possibly the most draining of our distraction mechanisms. When designed, the most popular apps were intended to make our connections easier, our lives more enriched, our time more productive. Social media has created more billionaires around this trend than in any one period in history. It has also created a legion of those who, instead of embracing this power source (and using it for the incredible tool it is), have allowed it to create a limited world in which they are now held captive. Here is where the discipline associated with a power break comes in. A power break is when you totally disconnect from any and everything tethered to social media for a predetermined block of time.

Dream Stealer #3: Television

One of the most powerful distractions that exists, the distraction that is so deadly due to its power to lull you into putting down even your most important work, stopping dreams in their tracks, is none other than **television.**

This is the device designed to give us that much-needed *occasional* dose of entertainment and to keep us updated on world events. However, this distraction tends to make you place your dreams on hold while watching others live theirs out.

> *Mind Shift*: The way to enjoy your occasional program without being robbed of your focus and result-oriented action is to give yourself a time slot to watch that program as a reward for completing a certain number of critical action items or tasks that drive your dreams or goals. I have a mantra that I live by regarding the television: "I won't watch a program on television until I am as successful in my own right as the actor or actress on that program is in their world." You decide which will get more of your time: your dreams, or that box?

Dream Stealer #4: Clutter

Clutter is the pickpocket in the realm of dream stealers. If your space is cluttered, your mind is then cluttered, preventing you from achieving the clarity you need to seize the opportunities that will transform your world. Clutter eases up on you in that stealthy way only clutter can, and then it takes your goals, dreams, and plans right out of your hands.

We give this crafty thief the ability to rob us when we fail to organize our living and workspaces. Clutter in these two key areas soon leads to clutter in other key areas of your life. This failure leads to a **cycle of distraction** that at its core has you starting a task and then becoming distracted by something in your line of sight that should have been organized and out of the way. The crazy thing is that for those who live this way, it has become such a way of life that they can't see the distractions and consider it normal.

Clutter is paralyzing in that it cuts you off from the critical visual cues needed to grow and evolve. It is here that the definition of insanity comes into play: doing the same things while expecting different results. This is also an area where it is incredibly difficult for most to admit they have an issue. My fellow Giants, if we are in denial of the change needed, we cut off the most incredible possibilities that will turn dreams into reality, not grasping that this is the most pivotal of moments. Giants understand that to reach a level of extreme clarity, we must understand the critical need to declutter the space around us.

> *Mind Shift*: Clutter must be eradicated before you can ever hope to assume your place among GIANTS. In order to clear clutter, you first must deal with the behavior that leads to the clutter. A simple fix is a mind shift that allows the development of a systematic action plan that ensures you will immediately put things away—from paperwork and books to clothing, and any other items that cause the space around you to become a breeding ground for distraction from the ideas and plans that will go on to transform your life. You will be amazed at how your productivity soars once you adapt this new mind shift.

Who Is Stealing Your Time?

Now that we have covered WHAT steals most of your time, crippling your chances of living your dreams, let's cover WHO is responsible for stealing your time, the distractions they cause, and how they work to kill your dreams.

Dream Stealer #5: Family and Friends

There's nothing on the planet that can derail your dreams like close family and friends. From the very inception of your dream, through every phase of its manifestation to its incredible evolution and results, your family and friends will test you far more than any other. In the most ambivalent way, the universe has decided to play a sad, cruel joke on those who desire their absolute best. That joke being that those you love most, those you would kill and die for, those you dream of benefiting from your dream lifestyle, are the very people who will sabotage you from the day you share your life-changing plan. The first and most painful blow is when you share your dreams only to hear from those you crave support from the most that it is impossible and to not quit your day job.

The road to living your dreams will inevitably run through family and friends. It will not get any easier as you intensify setting aside the time needed to pursue making real those audacious dreams. Family and friends feel entitled to so much of you. They are used to you giving so much of yourself, time and energy that now must be redirected, focused on the few things that will make your vision real and transform your life.

> *Mind Shift*: You will decide to take a firm stance here and now on your new hierarchy of priorities. Every Giant realizes they must, or they will say goodbye to their dreams and live a life of regret. This is a moment of growth that you will endure, and yes, it will change some relationships. You must make the decision to be a little selfish and not feel bad about it so you can create the life you envision. Make the decision today.

DREAM MAKER OR DREAM STEALER

Here is where you decide which of the two you will be—a decision every Giant before you has had to make. The extraordinary example of a dream maker, or the example of what it looks like to have your dreams crushed and die inside of you.

MAKING DREAMS REAL THROUGH TIME MANAGEMENT

The decisions you make around how you use your time will dictate how you spend the rest of your life. Giants understand that the moment you respect the laws governing time and realize you have the ultimate power and last say-so regarding your response to any request of your time, it is then that you unleash the power that determines the fate of your dreams.

PILLAR TWO
HIGH PERFORMANCE LEVELS

Giants understand you are only as good as the team around you. If you show me a poor team, then I will show you dismal results. Show me a good team, and I will show you okay results. You show me a High-Performance Team, and I will show you the makeup of every incredible act or great moment you will ever experience. Every Giant understands you do nothing phenomenal without a HIGH-PERFORMANCE TEAM!

Creating, nurturing, and maintaining a team of this caliber is easier said than done. If it were as easy as it sounds, we would all be living our dreams. For those who have attempted to put together or be part of a high-performance team, you may also know this can be a daunting process, but the payoff and results are priceless.

Before we work to construct your high-performance team, I first need to be assured we all understand the difference between a group, a team, and a high-performance team. Everything you will build and create going forward depends on understanding this.

A GROUP is simply a collection of people or things that are in the same space, same time for a reason. They all want the same team to win, they all want to protest the same issue, they all love the artist they came to hear . . . but that is where the affiliation ends.

A TEAM is a group of people interdependent with respect to information, resources, and skills who share a common purpose and several challenging goals. A team combines their efforts to achieve those goals. Without a purpose and goals, you cannot build a team.

HIGH-PERFORMANCE TEAMS

High-Performance Teams are at the very essence and core of every Giant. It is one of the dynamics that creates the phenomenal and amazing acts that allow the Giant results others only dream about. I need for you to really grasp that the universe has been designed it so you can do nothing incredible alone. Yes, that means in order to live your dream and walk into your destiny, you will have to create and nurture not a group (anyone can do that and get back group results), and not a team (which can get you results, but not those that manifest dreams into reality). No, for you to become a Giant and live like the extraordinary beings we were created to be, to go out and do the incredible, you will need to create a High-Performance Team.

The difference is staggering when you weight the results created from a high-performance team versus any other team or group on the planet. A high-performance team is a group of people with very specific roles and complementary talents and skills aligned with and committed to a purpose. These team members consistently show high levels of collaboration and innovation, produce superior results, and extinguish radical or extreme opinions that could be damaging. The high-performance team is regarded as tight knit, focused on their goal, and they have supportive processes in place that will enable every team member to surmount all barriers in achieving the team's goals. In other words, when assembled correctly and nurtured properly, a high-performance team is unstoppable. A high-performance team will deliver the incredible and ensure that you walk like the Giant you were created to be.

MINDSET

The success of high-performance teams starts and ends with mindset. In an ordinary team, the mindset is to win. Winning is good enough. In high-performance teams, the mindset is that of a champion: not simply to win but to dominate, to impose will, to set new benchmarks while becoming the standard of excellence in whatever the endeavor. High-performance teams allow you to turn the impossible into the incredible. The mindset is the objective without fail; it will be done! Excuses are nonexistent. Procrastination is not tolerated. The hurdles that cripple and stop most will inspire the high-performance team to dig deeper, to depend on and trust one another more, and in doing so transform the would-be hurdle into a springboard to even greater heights.

CULTURE

The culture of high-performance teams is the stuff dreams are made of. Culture at the high-performance level is the unique environment or incubator that nurtures, grows, and allows dreams to go from conception to manifestation. It encapsulates the values, characteristics, and critical overall attitude of an individual and/or group. That attitude is critical because it drives how we act and react to the many sacrifices, lessons, pain, and fire that is a part of our evolution from mere men and women to our place as Giants. That attitude will more than any other be the driving factor in your ultimate success or failure.

This unique culture is first one of individual strengths, blending to become collectively unstoppable. Most members of a high-performance team feel excited and satisfied to work on a collaborative team. They feel it is rewarding on so many levels to be asked and challenged to contribute at their highest level while also learning so much. On an average or good team, weakness is acceptable. High-performance teams work and thrive on magnifying times ten every strength, while turning every weakness into a strength. Great high-performance teams pride themselves on having no weak links. This is accomplished by making sure certain characteristics are in place at a very high level: Trust, Freedom of Expression, Clarity, Individual Performance, Disagreement and Conflict, Decisions, and Mutual Respect.

Trust

Team members have a solid and deep trust and they believe in the team purpose.

Freedom of Expression

Team members feel free to express ideas, feelings, and thoughts.

Clarity

There will be a level of clarity allowing those who get it to reach incredible heights. Most will never see the opportunities they can bring about because they are so caught up in what they don't have instead of looking at what the moment presents. Clarity at this level also allows goals to be accomplished with dazzling efficiency and mastery.

Individual Performance

Every team member works on an individual level to contribute their max at the team level.

Disagreement and Conflict

Disagreement is seen as a good thing and conflicts are managed.

Decisions

Decisions are made as a team. The high-performance team then distinguishes itself by having a single-minded focus: to ACCOMPLISH THE GOAL! That single-minded focus is centered around . . .

Mutual Respect

Of all the dynamics that hold together and drive a high-performance team, without mutual respect, none of the others can click to create the magic that allows teams to walk like Giants. That mutual respect is composed of:

Dependability: To know you can count on that person next to you without fail is the benchmark of all high-performance teams.

Adaptability: The best of the best high-performance teams are those that are able to adapt on a level that gives the team a clear-cut competitive edge. That adaptability gives the team confidence that fosters resilience in the face of obstacles, adversity, and change, making them unstoppable.

Flexibility: The flexibility of a high-performance team starts long before the team is ever formed. It is a characteristic of each person that makes up such a team. As a high-performance team, the ability to be flexible first as an individual and then at the team level makes it possible to perform and execute, creating game-changing results.

Now that you have the individual components, blend them into the five stages of the High-Performance Team Development Process. Bruce Tuckman, an educational psychologist, identified a five-stage development process that most teams follow to become high performing. The development stages are forming, storming, norming, performing, and adjoining.

Forming: The process of assembling the team. Everyone is positive and polite as they feel each other out. Team members and their mindset are essential to the eventual success or failure of the team.

Storming: With any team that has multiple type A personalities, conflict is inevitable. It is here that teams with insane potential to accomplish the incredible disintegrate. The key here is to respect differences. Understanding along with mutual respect are what will get you past this stage, and from here, the real magic happens.

Norming: Where the work pays off and you fall into a rhythm of working at a high performance level. It is here that you understand you have a special team, a team predicated on a single-minded focus, respect for differences, flexibility, and adaptability. It is here that goals start to fall, and real high-level growth takes place.

Performing: This is the stage at which you hit the level of true high performance. The team is in sync as few can be, you are moving past what you thought was possible, and in the process, you are creating new base lines. It is here you are recognized by those around you as a High-Performance Team.

Adjoining: At this point, for all the right reasons, the team is disassembled, allowing individual team members to go out with the growth and lessons learned to conquer and accomplish.

If you want to live your dreams, see, do, and create the extraordinary. If you want to walk like the Giant you were created to be, then understand and never lose sight of the fact that you will only go, do, and achieve up to the level of the team around you. It's simple—if you want incredible results, it will take an incredible team. Do this and you don't just realize, you surpass. Don't do this and don't respect this law of Giants, and you doom yourself to an average life and regret.

PILLAR THREE
PERSONAL DEVELOPMENT

The single component that carries more weight than any other in deciding if you live your best life versus one of regret is your level of commitment to your personal investment and development!

So many of us want the extraordinary, phenomenal lifestyle

and accolades we see others living, but we want it without paying the incredible price others payed to live that life.

If you ever hope to live your most incredible life, then you will have to at some point adapt the habit of the uber successful. This starts with investing and developing the five areas that will equate the amount of work and sacrifice you are willing to make as you become the best version of yourself you were designed and destined to be.

The five areas of personal development are physical, emotional, social, spiritual, and intellectual.

Physical is so critical because where your health goes, so do your dreams and plans. Make enough money and you can buy almost anything. Unfortunately, you cannot buy your health. That means taking care of your body is your responsibility. You will find as you navigate through life that the body will treat you as well or poorly as you treat it.

Your emotional development is the driving factor behind your mindset and attitude. Your mindset and attitude are and will be the driving factor behind ultimate success or failure.

Social skills are imperative as you work to evolve and transform your version of yourself and your life. Your ability to interact with others is key.

Spiritual refers to your spiritual beliefs, your faith, and tying those spiritual beliefs into your overall development.

Your intellectual development is vital to your overall personal development because it goes directly into what you feed your brain and how you process it.

A master was strolling through a field of wheat when a disciple came up to him and asked, "I can't tell which is the true path. What's the secret?"

"What does that ring on your right hand mean?" asked the master.

"My father gave it to me before dying."

"Well, give it to me."

The disciple obeyed, and the master tossed the ring into the middle of the field of wheat.

"Now what?" shouted the disciple. "Now I have to stop everything to look for the ring! It's important to me!"

"When you find it, remember this: you yourself answered the question you asked me. This is how you tell the true path. It is more important than all the rest."

"Decide your priority and you decide your path."

CHAPTER 4

PSYCHOLOGY 101

All that you are, every extraordinary thing that you will ever do, evolves and springs forth from one powerhouse source: your **mindset**.

Mindset is the difference between GIANTS and everyone else on the planet. Giants understand that in order to succeed at this level, the mindset evolves and is maintained within its ultimate support system: YOUR ENVIRONMENT.

As a GIANT, you can execute performance dynamics at an insane level. You are able to turn the impossible into the incredible, to live like others never will, because the **process** of creating and maximizing your environment allows you to live consistently those essential elements that most only ever tap occasionally or simply not at all. That means your environment totally supports your dreams with a lifestyle that at its most authentic and organic supports, promotes, and allows you to manifest your destiny.

The essential elements of the environment that creates, supports, and produces the mindset that manifests your destiny, that allows you to walk like the GIANT you were created to be, are:

- Self-Discipline
- Personal Development
- Habits
- Execution
- Performance
- Stimuli

The six elements that make up your game-changing environment can be further broken down into two categories. This will help you understand how they work in tandem to become the powerhouse source they were designed to be. The powerhouse source that makes you extraordinary. The powerhouse source that makes you a GIANT!

SELF-DISCIPLINE AND HABITS ARE ESSENTIAL TO YOUR PERSONAL DEVELOPMENT

Self-discipline is the bedrock of GIANTS! At the CORE of all that you ever hope to create, that you crave to evolve, is self-discipline. Along with BELIEF and DESIRE, it makes up the epicenter of your foundation. Your repeated actions produce the patterns that become HABITS. That self-discipline and those habits go on to influence and shape every facet of your lifestyle, the quality of your life, and how you WALK LIKE A GIANT!

Just what is self-discipline? Self-discipline is a phrase we often hear, but I can promise you most have no idea how important those two words are in relation to the goals you want to reach, the dreams you want to live out, and the overall quality of your life.

To have self-discipline, my friends, is to have self-love. It is by far the hardest thing you will ever have to do, and like excellence, it is not an act but an ongoing habit. It is having the ability to block out all distractions and resist all temptation, to deny yourself when every fiber of your being is crying out for what is good in the moment but detrimental to your dreams and goals. Self-discipline is not an act but a process. You will have those days where you are weak and cave in. The trick is to have more of the disciplined days than the undisciplined. Warren Buffett said that in order to separate yourself from the masses, to win the day and live your dreams, you don't have to be smarter than the rest, but you do have to be more disciplined.

Self-discipline comes down to doing what you need to do so you drive every thought, every action, every result toward not just looking at your dreams, nor just living them, but surpassing them.

"You are responsible for your place and your fate. The instant you control your discipline, you control your destiny."

THE HARDEST THING YOU WILL EVER DO

Self-discipline is not easy. If it were, we would all be living our dreams. We all know what we need to do, but doing it is a different matter. The difference between looking at your dreams and living them comes down not to the complex, but to simply having a greater desire than temptation and weakness.

There are no quick fixes here. No easy way through the trial by fire of discipline. Just this. The time for weakness is over. The time for excuses has passed. All you want is within your grasp. You will succeed in direct proportion to your level of discipline. Mind over everything is your test. The question is, are you getting up when it is cold out and those covers call you back? Are you putting in work when you don't feel like it? Working out when you don't want to? Eating the healthy choice versus the junk that is calling you? Will you have the discipline to put in the work that will allow you to live your dreams, or will you regret not having it the rest of your life?

Society has created a culture where expectations cater to weakness, to carnal cravings, to our lazy habits. The healthy choices, the right choices, are more expensive, are painful, and take extreme work, whereas it is so easy to give in to what's fast, easy, and lazy. Understanding the immediate fix wreaks havoc on our bodies, our brains, and ultimately, our dreams.

This book would have forever been just a dream and never made it into your hands to create the intended change had I not wanted it badly enough and become disciplined in so many areas. I had to make the decision that at some point every Champion, every one who has ever experienced greatness, every GIANT, has had to make—I had to decide to dedicate my life to a lifestyle that supported my dreams. I had to decide that those dreams were so important to me I would make every and any change necessary to live my absolute best life.

HABITS ARE KING

Over and over, you do it without even realizing. That little jump in place when you're excited, stroking your hair when talking to your girlfriends, scratching your head when baffled, closing your eyes tight for a second before you take a leap of faith. These are all actions that are automatic because they have become ingrained habits. They are as much a part of you as breathing. Habits, therefore, are those actions carried out without any conscious thought of the act itself. You are and will forever evolve from the sum of your actions. Actions that on a small scale go almost unnoticed. Your standard of living, your opportunities, your rewards and pitfalls are all a direct result of your repeated actions, your habits. Actions that on a larger scale are so impactful because they influence your quality of life on every level and, in fact, become the tipping point that decides if you live the life of dreams or a life of regret.

Most of us have developed far more bad habits or we have failed to develop good ones. Those habits have become the very walls standing between you and all that you want, all that you dream of, all that you will ever become. To become the person you want to become, the person you were destined to become you pay a price. The question is how high of a price are you willing to pay.

CONSCIOUS AND UNCONSCIOUS HABITS

An example of a conscious habit is leaving home an hour early for appointments so that you are always early. Giving yourself a power talk before walking into a room or event. Reading for thirty minutes to an hour every day. Each is an investment in yourself. An example of an unconscious habit is putting your feet up when you read, or a fist pump when you do something incredible. Popping your gum while chewing.

The GIANT excels because they are aware that any habit, conscious or unconscious, can be changed. It is critical that you understand this, because so many live lives of misery due to never employing the discipline to change the habits that drive the results in their lives.

At certain points in your evolution, a self-assessment comes due. Those assessments, if honest, will unveil how you are living and where changes should be made in the form of tweaking habits, from getting up earlier to more focus during that reading time.

EXECUTION AND STIMULI ARE ESSENTIAL ELEMENTS OF PERFORMANCE

If you get nothing else, I need for you to get this. At some point, every Giant, as a part of the evolutionary process that takes you from who you are to who you are destined to be, will go through a series of aha moments. Light will shine where there was only darkness. Clarity will shine where there had only been murkiness. Of these moments, none are as profound as realizing no one but you and I, the individual in us, decides our fate. That fate is decided not by how much we think or plan, but your fate and my fate are ultimately decided by our level of **execution**. Everything you will ever become, do, or create is tied directly to how well you execute. We all have the dream, the plan, or goal; this is the level where we find out who amongst us will live those dreams and who will live a life of regret. The law of Giants within the psychology of CORE DYNAMICS states that whatever your level and at whatever stage you presently reside, you are there first and foremost because of your mindset and ability to execute. It is said, "If you want different results, you must enact different actions." This is the basis of the psychology of Core Dynamics.

The other compelling reason that we don't excel, that we don't reach goals, that we don't realize our dreams, is we don't understand the power of **execution**. It is this simple—you execute, you see the results in the evolution of your lifestyle. Fail to execute and your life becomes one of regret. We will talk more about execution in chapter 6.

STIMULI

Stimuli are the things around you that combine to act as a catalyst, that fuel the incredible level of execution at the Giant level. They are critical because they directly impact your level of commitment to execute. Stimuli are the people, places, and things that influence your mood, mindset, and energy.

Don't wait until everything is just right. It will never be perfect. There will always be challenges, obstacles, and less than perfect conditions. So, what. Get started now. With each step you take, you will grow stronger and stronger, more and more skilled, more and more self-confident, and more and more successful.

—Mark Victor Hansen

CHAPTER 5

THE FOUNDATION

To live, to TRULY live, we must be willing to RISK. To be nothing in order to find everything. To leap before we look.

—Mandy Hale
The Single Woman: Life, Love, and a Dash of Sass

Richard Turere as a twelve-year-old was very unique. He lives in Nairobi National Park in Kenya. The animals in this park are free to roam, including lions. The lions presented quite the problem in that they often killed the livestock in Richard's village.

Richard decided he wanted to help solve this problem. He first tried fire, only to have it light the way to the livestock. He next tried a scarecrow. It worked for all of a day before the smart lions figured out it was not alive and had their way with the livestock. On his next try, he hit pay dirt. He discovered lions are afraid of moving light. He devised a circuit of blinking lights that, once in place, solved the village's problem with the lions for good.

His invention earned him a scholarship to the best college in Kenya and also a TED Talk.

Keep your dreams alive. Understand to achieve anything requires faith and belief in yourself, vision, hard work, determination, and dedication. Remember all things are possible for those who believe.

—Gail Devers

Chapter 5 introduces Giant Nation to the components that make up the most important element in the makeup of a Giant: FOUNDATION. If you don't read any other chapter but this one, you will understand how Giants are able from the core to create the unique, game-changing FOUNDATION that allows for "Surpassing Dreams, Realizing Destiny!" Foundation is the bedrock that supports the epicenter of Core Dynamics. In other words, that foundation supports all that you are, all that you do, and all that you hope to be. You are only as good as your foundation is strong. Even more important is that foundation is the lifeline of every Giant. Understand that as we do life at extreme levels, we will at some point be tested, knocked to our knees by life. It is here you find two kinds of people. The first person is that person who got knocked down, the foundation underneath so weak and cracked it could not support their getting back up. That person's dream died that day, and they would have, should have, could have ten years later.

The other person also gets knocked down to their knees. The difference is they have a phenomenal foundation underneath fortified by multiple layers. That person's strong foundation is made up of layers upon layers of the coaching, mentoring, advice, confidence, wisdom, evolution, and experiences that allow you to move with focus. The entire premise of this program, once you've committed to the process, allows you to have in place the FOUNDATION OF A GIANT. This foundation is the difference between average and exceptional. It will contain the following elements.

SELF-ACCEPTANCE/SELF-LOVE

Most of us never realize our brilliance because we hate ourselves. We hate and are ashamed of past mistakes. We can't hope to sell others on our dreams when we can't even convince and sell ourselves. The most powerful version of yourself is born the instant you accept your now, wherever you are, and you forgive yourself for past mistakes, understanding that you are stronger, better, wiser because of those mistakes. Your past has invaluable lessons that will benefit you in your future. Love who you are!

FORGIVENESS

It is simple; you are not nor will you ever be perfect. That means at some point you will have to forgive yourself. And forgive others for the hurt you have endured along the way. Hurt that is not released will hold you hostage to your dreams.

A PLAN/GOAL/DREAM CLEARLY DEFINED

Without a plan, your dream does not exist. Without goals, there is no discipline or direction and you simply drift. Without dreams that are clearly defined, your core reason for enduring the tears, pain, and hard times associated with living your dreams becomes clouded, making it easy for you to quit when your journey gets rough.

SELF-DISCIPLINE

To have SELF-DISCIPLINE, my friends, is to have self-love. It is by far the hardest process you will ever go through. Like excellence, it is not an act but an ongoing habit. Self-discipline is having the ability to block out all distractions and resist all temptation, to deny yourself when every fiber of your being is crying out for what is good in the moment but detrimental to your dreams and goals.

YOUR CIRCLE

Even more critical than the habits that help shape your destiny are the people that make up your inner circle. Those people help shape your world. Your circle starts at an outer mark and from there comes in until you have your most intimate circle. It is so very true. If you want to see the direction in which a person is moving simply look at the five people within their inner circle or the five people, the spend the most time with. 100% without fail their life will mimic in microcosmic patterns the lives of those five closest to them. One of the most profound Laws of Giants is that if you want to change your life, change your circle. Simple but powerful!

TIME MANAGEMENT

Where time is concerned, Giants understand that how we use our time is one powerful way to control our destiny, and not simply leave it to chance.

PERSONAL INVESTMENT AND SELF-DEVELOPMENT

Giants are different in that they understand you only create the type of foundation that allows you to do things most will never be able to do by investing in themselves like most of us won't.

CREATING A HIGH-PERFORMANCE TEAM

Giants get to live extraordinary lives because they understand the concept that you surround yourself with those smarter, faster, and better in areas where you lack certain high-level skill sets. This group comprises the high-performance team responsible for transforming your dreams into your destiny.

MINDSET

There is no other mindset like the mindset of a Giant. It is unmatched and unbeatable. It is that mindset that will ultimately allow you to reach goals and surpass dreams. It is that mindset that will push you past every perceived limit and every one of your fears; it is what gets you over hurdles and makes sure you survive your worst days. That mindset is focused and dedicated to the sole purpose and reason every Giant exists. To never simply exist but to always thrive, to be their most authentic, audacious, bold, and daring selves while evolving, making imprints that are game and life changing. All of this is made possible by the extraordinary level of mindset found within each and every Giant on the planet.

PERFORMANCE

The Law of Giants states that to merely call yourself Giant is not enough. The title is never given; like an Olympic champion, it is earned. Earned by your Herculean efforts, consistent performance at insane levels, and game-changing, record-breaking results.

EXECUTION

A Giant can execute at such an insanely high level, manifesting incredible results, and live lives most only dream about due to their evolved ability to apply choice and execute.

Once you make the conscious decision to apply a level of commitment you have never applied before, understanding that to get what you never had, you must do what you have never done, what brings it all together and takes you from looking at to living your dreams is high-level execution.

EMBRACING CHANGE

The evolution of change is one of the most painful, trying, and challenging processes you will ever endure. Change hurts on every level. It goes against whatever is present. In order to build a muscle, you must challenge yourself to pick up weights that will try you. Work that muscle group until it has been pushed, and then over the coming days endure the pain of that muscle contracting as it goes through the painful metamorphosis of growth. On the other side of that pain is discovery and growth and you living your dreams. You "WALKING LIKE A GIANT."

BELIEF

Absolute belief is the cornerstone in the foundation of every Giant. It is the single determining dynamic, the X factor, the degree of separation that vaults those who absolutely believe to unthinkable awards, accolades, and a life surpassing every dream. Yet so many fall short, not understanding they will be tested. When your belief is put to fire, only those who walk through will live their dream, while those who don't see their dreams consumed by that very fire.

ATTITUDE

Do you walk into a room thinking you are unbeatable, or that you might be beaten? Do you think you are unstoppable, or that you might just be stopped? The answer to that question determines if your attitude is that of someone average or that of a Giant.

CHAPTER 6

THE APPLICATION! THE EXECUTION!

Excellence is an art won by training and habituation. We do not act rightly because we have virtue or excellence, but we rather have those because we have acted rightly. We are what we repeatedly do. Excellence, then, is not an act but a habit.

— Aristotle

Amy Purdy, Game Changer!

I found the following story from AmyPurdy.com that shows the never-quit attitude all Giants possess:

Amy Purdy has gone from a girl just hoping to snowboard again to global icon. Amy, like most game changers, begins this story with a set of circumstances that would have broken most. As a teen, Amy Purdy ate, slept, and breathed snowboarding. She was happy-go-lucky and had the world at her feet . . . then life happened. She fell suddenly very ill and doctors soon found that she had bacterial meningitis. They saved her life but had to amputate her legs below the knee. She also lost her spleen and had partial loss of hearing.

She was in a coma for months. Coming out of the coma, she made a decision that would both save and change her life. Amy decided she had to at all costs get back on a snowboard. Driven by sheer passion, seven months later she had done just that. "When you are passionate about something, nothing can stop you," she says. At the time, there were not prosthetic legs that would allow her to get on a board, so she and her doctor designed and made one.

Today, Amy is a world champion, having won three World Cup gold medals in adaptive snowboarding. She has a nonprofit company that promotes new life for amputees, she has done *Dancing with the Stars,* and she has a life-changing TED talk. As you explore this chapter on new shoes and finding new footing, think about Amy—a GIANT! A Game Changer!

"A Giant does one thing better than anyone on the planet— they EXECUTE! They understand that to wallow in the anger, pain, despair, or challenging issues of the moment is to allow those distractions to rob you of your best, most audacious, most authentic self."

Most will never master the dynamic duo of performance and execution that is a must-have in making dreams real, because first they allow their time to be drained; next, distractions dim their clarity, killing any momentum; and most critical of all, they never admit to having a problem in those areas.

I am a believer that at some point we all get tired of being tired. It is there, when we hit the wall that every Giant hits, that we make and began to apply the decisions every Giant makes and commits to. That decision: to no longer allow anything to stand between themselves and living their dream. At some point, looking at the dream daily is no longer substantial. At some point, you have to either live it or watch as a part of you dies off, leaving you a shell of the person you once were.

Execution is easy to talk about, but extremely difficult for most to apply. The keys to consistent execution and living life at a high level starts with these fundamentals.

IDENTIFY YOUR ONE THING

Most people on the planet fail to execute and ever see major plans and dreams realized because they have so many things in front of them. This has two devastating effects. First, it robs you of the clarity that uberproducers utilize allowing them to see and take advantage of opportunities in the moment. That clarity is the dynamic that separates greatness from average. The other effect is that because they attempt to attack so many things at the same time, they end up not doing anything that produces game-changing results at the level we need to make dreams real—a high level.

The answer is to only focus on the one thing you want to accomplish now. You support that by cutting out everything but the focal points and activities that drive the accomplishment of that dream or plan. Once you accomplish that one, then you move on to the next one with the same, intense laser focus. That, my fellow Giants, is how Giants get it done.

DEVELOP A PLAN

To keep your focus at an uber level and accomplish the incredible, you need a plan. A plan allows you to wake up and move throughout your day with direction. This direction is key! The steps to implement this direction are:

SHARPENING YOUR FOCUS

Sharper focus involves allowing into your circle less of the things and people that cripple your clarity, and more of the things and people that awaken and allow that clarity to peak. It is at that peak state you separate yourself from others. It is at this peak state you see opportunities others just can't. It is at this state your mental processes are power driven.

EMBRACING NO

So many of us will never live out our dreams simply because we are not disciplined with our time. You will, as you evolve through the stages of becoming the Giant you are destined to be, learn one thing, or never have chance at living your dream. This one thing you learn is how critical it is to embrace saying no to everyone and everything outside your dream.

ESTABLISING PROCESSES TO MEASURE RESULTS

If you do not have processes in place to measure your results and hold you accountable to a minimum standard, you, my friend, are not serious about attaining your goals. This means there is no way you can be serious about living like a Giant.

ASSESSING CONSTANTLY WHERE YOU ARE

You should have some assessment of where you are and how you are progressing by having some process in place to measure progress.

TWEAKING YOUR PLAN

By having processes in place that measure results and where you are currently trending, you are able to tweak your plan and not just look at your dreams, but do what so few can: live those dreams.

KEEP IT MOVING

The worst feeling in the world is to think back and wish you had stayed with something, not quit, not let go, not give in and make a permanent decision based on temporary circumstances. Anyone with the heart of a champion and walk of a Giant understands that you don't stop, you don't quit, you don't give in, and no matter what, you KEEP IT MOVING!

PUSHING THROUGH

Every Giant on the planet has certain traits inbred in their DNA. One key trait in every Giant is the ability to push through. There are times when we are human and decide we just don't want to do it today, be it getting up, working, working out, eating right, or working on our craft. The difference is that most will cave in, take that time off, and not get it done—staying in bed longer, not working, not working out, not working on their craft. Excuses are made, weakness justified, and complaints put out to all who will listen about how we hate our current life. The Giant, however, has an internal voice and gear that compels them to not only push through the urge to be average, but in those moments to excel. It is these moments where most lie down that Giants push through to become icons.

"The greater danger for most of us lies not in setting our aim too high and falling short, but in setting our aim too low and achieving our mark."

—Michelangelo

Do you know that an eagle knows when a storm is approaching long before it breaks? The eagle will fly to some high spot and wait for the winds to come. When the storm hits, it sets its wings so the wind will pick it up and lift it above the storm. While the storm rages below, the eagle is soaring above it. The eagle does not escape the storm; it simply uses the storm to lift it higher. It rises on the winds that bring the storm.

When the storms of life come upon us, like the eagle, we can rise above them and ride the winds of the storm that bring sickness, tragedy, failure, and disappointment into our lives.

What is your greatest challenge right now? Jot it down. And then, let it lift you higher.

CHAPTER 7

THE ULTIMATE SALE!
SELLING YOURSELF TO YOURSELF AND OTHERS

The sale is always there; the question and evolution come in understanding when you are selling and when you are being sold.

I love every chapter in this book, but I have to admit this is the one I am most excited about. Why? Because the Law of Giants states that you can master every other dynamic and strategy in this book, but if you don't recognize and become proficient at this one skill, you will never realize your dreams or become the Giant you were destined to be.

There are three critical factors that keep most of us from living our dreams. The first is an attitude that lacks confidence and belief in ourselves and our ability to make our dreams real. The second reason so many dreams never see their potential or die inside of us is the lack of consistent, focused execution. Then, there is the reason that snatches more dreams, but that most never consider a reason for failure until that internal fire has been extinguished. That thing is the ability to SELL!

The act of **sales** is something we all do daily. Something we do without even realizing it, because we do it as naturally as we breathe. I know you have heard this countless times, so I will give you the unique perspective of Giants. Think about this concept. If you are living, then you are in sales. We have all been selling since we came out of the womb. Our first sale ever was us selling our parents that if they provide milk and a dry diaper, we in turn would be quiet. This sales relationship evolved as we got older. Our parents, in turn, sold us on the belief that eating the foods we hated and getting decent grades would lead to strong, healthy bodies, healthy bodies that would enable us to pursue our definition of success. We make other sales daily, on programs we want to watch, what we want for to plans and outings, and so on. Throughout our day, someone is selling and someone is being sold. We all possess this raw ability to sell. The fork in the road that separates the Giants from average comes with deciding to hone that selling skill set. If those skills are not honed and elevated, our dreams don't stand a chance and will surely die inside us.

THE ACT OF SELLING

The average person will SELL TO LIVE, but the best in the world in any arena, those who live their dreams daily, are those who LIVE TO SELL! They understand the need to sell at a high level. They also have figured out there is a technique and a formula to selling at a level that, if practiced consistently, changes your life. While there are many sales formulas out there, the one I have used and find highly effective is a seven-step formula you will find below:

1. Establish a rapport with your potential customer, creating a dialogue that allows you to find a common ground.
2. Build trust so that you now have a kinship with the other person. In most cases, they can buy the same product from any number of people. They buy from you because of the relationship and the trust established.
3. Listen to determine a want, need, or a problem. Here's where you stop talking and listen—listen to what the other person wants, needs, or what problem

you can help them solve. Solve that problem, and you have that sale and a customer for life!

4. Offer a solution and explain what you can do or how you can help get what they need or want.

5. Soft close (try at this point to close the sale) to test the waters, gauging if the other party is ready to buy into whatever you are selling be it an idea, an act, a product, or your dream.

6. Overcome objections. Any great salesperson understands that an objection does not mean no. It simply means you didn't explain some part of your solution so the other person has total buy-in. The other critical part of this is the other party must ALWAYS feel that they walk away with a WIN-WIN. Yes, you will get what you want out of the sale and the other party feels you care about them and are just as invested in their win as your own.

7. Close the sale. Here is where you come back around to the close, now confident that you have reexplained the value and benefits, how the other party has a WIN-WIN, and that they now have the total buy-in. You close here with a new friend or a stronger, deeper relationship with the other party.

That is the seven-step sales process that will allow you to fully engage in the act of selling.

THE ART OF SELLING

The art of selling has everything to do with the psychology of selling. The difference in those people who walk the earth doing average things, achieving average goals, living an average life, versus those who walk the earth as incredible Giants, doing extraordinary things, achieving extraordinary goals, living an extraordinary life, comes down to MINDSET!

The foundation of next-level sales of doing all of the incredible, life-changing, phenomenal things you want to do all tie into the psychology of MINDSET!

The way you approach the few critical areas in your life will without fail determines the quality of your life. Yes, what you do throughout the sale process matters, yet sales experts will tell you the sale is won or lost in your mental approach before the sale even starts. That approach includes . . .

SALES CLARITY

Having a very clear picture of what a great outcome around every sale looks like and what a win to both sides looks like. This allows you to . . .

BE PRESENT

If you want to increase your percentage of success in anything, but especially sales, you want to learn to be FULLY PRESENT! This means no matter how great or how terrible you did on the previous sale, it amounts to you taking the momentum of a great sale and moving on the next sale fully present. It also means when told no, not closing the sale, you don't taking it personally, instead learning the lesson of why and moving on. Don't dwell, but be fully present in the moment in this sale. This instantly tells whomever you are dealing with that they are important enough to have your undivided attention. To earn and keep their trust, to have them listen to you and ultimately close a deal with you on any level, they must see you are FULLY PRESENT.

DOING YOUR HOMEWORK

DO YOUR RESEARCH! Doing your homework means simply showing up to any selling situation knowing your product and your customers on a level most won't. This gives you the ability to close sales and do the incredible things most don't.

COMMITMENT TO WIN

The magic in sales occurs when both parties walk away feeling like they just made the best deal ever. The instant you forget this principal is the moment you fail. You will forever win if you keep the other person first and make sure they walk feeling like they got a win.

Our destiny changes with our thought; we shall become what we wish to become, do what we wish to do, when our habitual thought corresponds with our desire.

—Orison Swett Marden

One example of one of the greatest pure sales Giants on the planet is Oprah Gail Winfrey.

Oprah Gail Winfrey has earned many titles, including most influential woman in the world, award-winning actress, media mogul, talk show queen, philanthropist, and first African American billionaire. She is one of the greatest examples that it is not how you start, but how you finish.

Born to a single mother, Oprah was raped at age nine. She became a single mom at age fourteen, her baby dying in infancy. She would endure hardship after hardship, all the while carving out a path that would take her to heights she never dreamed of. Oprah can tell this story and be an example because she never allowed anyone else to define her worth, and no matter what, always moved forward. She NEVER QUIT!

The rest, as they say, was history. If you want an example of starting out with seemingly everything against you, and brick by brick building a foundation that will support the amazing world you can go on to create, here you have it! So, tell me again, what's stopping you?

CHAPTER 8

CHANGE

Giant Nation, as of this moment, everything, and I do mean everything, in your world changes. You don't have a choice; you change, or your dreams will die. That simple. It is here your vision, your clarity, your attitude, your mindset, your concept of time all elevate to an insane level, while those things that combined previously to prevent you from living your dreams, you painfully wean yourself off of or redefine where they fit in your priorities. Who you become after today will be determined by your ability to grasp the concept that the person you are currently is not the same person you picture living your dreams. That person has gone through trial, through fire; that person has undergone tremendous change on every level.

Change is defined as the act or instance of becoming different. The evolution of change is one of the most painful, trying, and challenging processes you will ever endure. Change hurts on every level. It goes against whatever is present. In order to build a muscle, you must challenge yourself to pick up weights that will try you. Work that muscle group until it has been pushed, and then over the coming days, endure the pain of that muscle contracting as it goes through the painful metamorphosis of growth. On the other side of that pain is discovery and growth and you living your dreams. You WALKING LIKE A GIANT.

THE PSYCHOLOGY OF CHANGE

You, my fellow Giants, cannot expect to act differently or to live differently without, at your core, becoming different. Change is so fundamental, yet so feared. Feared because we as humans are, more than anything else, creatures of habit. We miss the mark in not realizing comfort zones are our absolute worst enemy. Where we should be fighting to destroy those comfort zones and complacency, we instead fight change and evolution with every fiber of our being.

The fight to hold on to comfort zones is so powerful, in fact, that failure to embrace change is one of the two chief reasons most of us will never live out our dreams or walk as Giants. In case you are curious, the other reason is lack of execution.

THE PROCESS OF CHANGE

Change, my fellow Giants, is the process that takes you from looking at your dreams to living them. Most will quit rather than endure this process that is like no other, relegating themselves to settle for a life of what could have been. But if seen through to the end, this transformation will reward you in ways you can't imagine.

YOU ARE NOT MOST! Everything you want is on the other side of change! This is the most tangible concept of the single most impactful process you will ever experience. That process—CHANGE!

The process of change is the most grueling and challenging of all. It is made up of multiple stages, each designed to force from you introspection, growth, and commitment and, if embraced, the lifestyle of Giants, surpassing your dreams and realizing your destiny.

The stages of change are:

1. Pain
   There are two types of pain: the pain that hurts, and the pain that alters. There are four dynamics in the process of pain. Allowing yourself to go through this process is

invaluable in both influencing your level of growth as well as producing a healthy, vibrant you coming out on the other side of that pain.

2. Introspection
    It is critical you find the quiet place that allows you to take a good, long, honest hard look at where you are, why you're experiencing pain, and what change is needed to fix this pressure point. This introspection is so important because your thought process and reasoning here will dictate where you go and what you look like at the next level.

3. Growth
    Growth is the byproduct of pain and introspection. The decisions made at this stage will dictate what you do and how you live going forward. Without this growth, you don't evolve. Without evolution, you stop dreaming, and at some point, instead start regretting. Growth is the cornerstone in the foundation of every Giant.

4. Commitment
    Commitment is so profoundly powerful because it is your promise to yourself. Your promise to do whatever is needed, to go through whatever the universe demands, so you evolve, elevate, and make Giant imprints in every area of your life.

5. The Other Side
    On the other side of the intense pain, the introspection, the growth, and commitment is everything you dream of, work for, cry over, and are destined and designed to be.

When it is ready, change will whisper to you. If not addressed, it will next tap you on the shoulder. When that doesn't work, it will shout, and then comes the pain as it slams into your life.

"You accept change, then adapt. You process, finding opportunity where there was none, turning the impossible into the incredible. That is the result of change when embraced."

Isaiah Bird, No Excuses!

Isaiah Bird doesn't have a leg to stand on or a place to call home, but on the wrestling mat he has the heart of a gladiator and an infectious smile that can bring even a UFC champion to his knees.

This six-year-old gladiator, who was born without legs, lives in a shelter in Freeport, New York, with his mother and two-year-old brother. The mountainous adversity thrown upon him could break any normal man, but there is something to be said about the pure and innocent heart of a child, yearning only to be happy.

"He has no clue what's going on in his life. He's such a happy kid that he doesn't know he doesn't have a bed, doesn't have a TV," said Miguel Rodriguez, Isaiah's wrestling coach, during an interview with Mark La Monica of *Newsday*. "Wrestling is the only thing this kid talks about. In wrestling, he can actually feel normal because he's the man."

Wrestling is often considered the great equalizer in all forms of athletic competition. It's a sport that isn't dictated by size, strength or natural athletic ability. It's a sport where anyone can be a giant or hero—regardless of how big they are.

The fact that Bird doesn't have legs is irrelevant when he's on the mat. He wears his singlet proud, like a shiny suit of armor draped over a modern-day warrior. For a moment in time, everything else in Isaiah's life fades away, and he is looked at and treated like every other kid.

He is viewed and treated as a gladiator.

"Yeah, I have no legs, but I don't need no legs. I'm a wrestler, I'm a gladiator," Bird told Island during a recent interview. GIANTS come in all sizes, but they all have one thing in common: HEART.

Prepare yourself, for now you are about to surpass dreams and realize your destiny. Change is not easy! If it were, everyone would live the life of their DREAMS. This chapter has created a portal that opens to your wildest, craziest, most audacious dreams. Now you will be eating, sleeping, and breathing this new lifestyle that is the gateway to all you have dreamed of, sought, and wanted. The life and the lifestyle that when you close your eyes and see yourself living starts the moment you embrace the change of mindset, the change of work ethic, the change of habits . . . the change, my fellow Giants, of all that must change to create the new version of you.

CHAPTER 9

TAKE YOUR FIRST GIANT STEP!

You are here, so open the door to your best! Your most amazing! Your most phenomenal! Open the door to your greatest, most insane life chapter ever! Realize that you are, with every step, Surpassing Dreams, Realizing Destiny.

There was a blind girl who hated herself just because she was blind. She hated everyone except her loving boyfriend. He was always there for her. She said if she could only see the world, she would marry her boyfriend.

One day, someone donated a pair of eyes to her, and then she could see everything, including her boyfriend. Her boyfriend asked her, "Now that you can see the world, will you marry me?"

The girl was shocked when she saw that her boyfriend was blind, too, and refused to marry him. Her boyfriend walked away in tears, and later wrote a letter to her saying:

"Just take care of my eyes, Dear."

Never forget those who sacrificed so you could take the steps of a GIANT.

The story for this chapter is one you will write. Here is where you thank someone who has believed in you, pushed you, carried and propelled you to levels you never thought possible.

This chapter begins wrapping up the book, but not our journey.

This is just the beginning. The book and I, David Lawhorn, will from now on be a lifelong friend. From here, there will be a steady flow of books, CDs, DVDs, and live programs to ensure each step is THAT OF A GIANT!

"Trust yourself. You know more than you think you do."

—Benjamin Spock

YOU

Here is where our journey together expands so you can put down this book, stop looking at your best life, and start living it. You will, from time to time, come back and reaffirm. You will add to this book others that I have in store, and I hope to meet you at one of my live events. Bring your book with you! I want to sign it for you.

YOU ARE READY!

You now stand where few have stood. On the threshold of taking your place as a Giant, of walking in the Land of Giants. This book has given you the strategies and tools, and honed your mindset—in fact, it has created a mind *shift* that is essential to your evolution as a Giant and all the rewards and lifestyle changes that come with the insane work and sacrifices you have undergone. You are now poised to take the impossible and do the incredible. To live, work, and play at levels most will only dream about.

This last chapter is all about you. From this day, you walk and live as a Giant. I want you to document your journey through journals. Find me an uber successful person on this planet, and you will find some form of journaling nearby. You will find that writing reinforces your strengths, allows an objective look at areas of opportunities, and most of all, is both freeing and confirming. You may have been writing, and if so, great. If not, you are about to start a habit you will carry out with love until your last breath.

Life is a gift—live it, enjoy it, celebrate it, and fulfill it. Live it to its fullest and you won't regret it. Don't and your last breath will be full of nothing but tears of regret.

—Erynn Louviaite, "Life Is a Gift"

This chapter is the first insert of the journal that is to mark the coming milestones and that you should keep as a reminder of who you are at your core. Your next ten GIANT STEPS will go here. You are ready; everything you need is there. I ask that you send me a copy of your chapter when it is written so I can share with the world and honor you . . . in the pantheon of GIANTS! The following pages are all yours. Welcome to the Land of Giants!

YOUR STORY
(CHAPTER 10 EXERCISE)

ACKNOWLEDGMENTS

Mom and Dad—I want to thank my parents, Joe and Delores Lawhorn, for the unwavering love and belief in me no matter the season of my life. For being my biggest fans, I thank and love you.

To my Earthly brother, Michael Lawhorn, I love and thank you for always being that rock that I can depend on. To my brother in heaven, Zeric Lawhorn, thank you for being my angel and forever pushing me. Love you both.

Mentors—Michelle Hanchey, you came into my life and from day one you have never stopped making me a better version of me. Thank you for your love, support, and for sharing all your knowledge and wisdom with me. Ken Westray, I will always believe that fate had us meet that day. Thank you for getting me to find and bring out the absolute best of myself. Your way of processing, sharing your keen business mind, and best practices can never be repaid. Thank you!

To Debbie Lawhorn—Debbie, you share my last name and we shared almost a decade together. You do and will always hold a uniquely special place in my world. I would not be the Giant I am today without you. Though we are no longer together, we will always be friends and I will always love you and celebrate you for never settling for less than my best, for putting up with and loving me through my worst, and for the numerous other things you have done that I can never repay. It would take a book to tell the world who you have been to me, for me, and with me, and how I will forever credit you for parts of my growth. Thank you!

David Lawhorn is founder and CEO of David Speaks International, an Atlanta, Georgia–based high-performance and elite execution think tank. After a stellar career in sales, in which he broke or set numerous national sales records, David transitioned to the role of corporate sales trainer, where again he and his sales teams went on to break and set national records. David, with his "Walking Like a Giant" mantra, is sought after both as a dynamic keynote speaker and game-changing performance trainer. He is obsessed with the psychology and mindset behind staggering performance and life-altering execution.

His client list includes Macy's, Siemens, CDC, T-Mobile, CarMax, IHG, and a host of others that make up GIANT NATION.

You can book David at www.Giantspeaks.com.